Learn About Scotland
Donald
The Hairy Coo

Join Donald as he shows you one of the best countries in the world.

By
A H Jamieson

Learn About Scotland With Donald The Hairy Coo

By A H JAMIESON

www.ahjamieson.com

Published by
Peerie Breeks Publishing,
6 Bridge St,
Kelso,
Scottish Borders,
TD5 7JD

© 2016 Peerie Breeks Publishing

All rights reserved. No portion of this book may be reproduced in any form without permission from the publisher, except as permitted by copyright law.

For permissions contact: ahjamiesonwriter@gmail.com

Hello,
my name is Donald. I am a hairy coo and I want to
tell you all about the fantastic place I live called
Scotland.

This map of Scotland is coloured
in blue because it's
our national
colour.

The thistle is our national flower.

One of the most beautiful sights in Scotland is the purple plant called heather which carpets the hills in colour.

Tartan is a pattern consisting of criss-crossed horizontal and vertical bands in lots of different colours.

It's a very special thing for us Scots.

What is this strange creature?
A spider?
A sea beast?

No!
It's a set of bagpipes! A special musical instrument.

This man is a piper.
He has spent a long time learning to play the bagpipes.

Do you know what he is wearing?

It's called a kilt. A special piece of Scottish tartan. Each Scottish family has their own special pattern.

Highland dancing is a style of competitive dancing. Often performed at the Highland games, where it is accompanied by bagpipe music.

Look at this steam train on the Glenfinnan viaduct. Is that Harry Potter I see?

A viaduct is a long bridge with lots of arches, carrying a road or railway across a valley.

Scotland is a place where people care about the environment and try to think of ways to look after it like these electricity producing wind turbines.

The Forth Rail Bridge.

For 125 years it has been an icon of engineering, excellence and a symbol of Scotland.
Now, the Forth Bridge has been granted Unesco World Heritage Site status, putting it alongside the Pyramids of Egypt, the great Wall of China and the Sydney Opera House in terms of cultural significance.

Sometimes the traffic can be crazy!

This is the Scottish Parliament in the capital city, Edinburgh.
Lots of important decisions are made here.

It's important because the Scottish people decide who gets to sit inside and make good choices for Scotland.

Inside the Parliament, seats are arranged in a circle so everyone can see and listen to each other more easily.

Robert Burns, also known as Rabbie Burns, the Bard of Ayrshire, was a Scottish poet and writer. He is widely regarded as the national poet of Scotland and is celebrated worldwide. He is the best known of the poets who have written in the Scots language.

He wrote 'Address to a Haggis'
Haggis is a savoury pudding containing sheep's heart, liver and lungs minced with onion, oatmeal, suet, spices, and salt, mixed with stock, traditionally encased in the animal's stomach.

You will have to take my word for it that it is delicious!

Fair fa' your honest, sonsie face,
Great chieftain o the puddin'-race!
Aboon them a' ye tak your place,
Painch, tripe, or thairm:
Weel are ye worthy o' a grace
As lang's my arm.

It is often eaten with neeps and tatties. (turnip and potato)

Then washed down with some Scottish Whiskey.

There are some amazing inventions to see. Like the Falkirk Wheel, a special machine to lift boats up and down from the Forth and Clyde Canal and the Union Canal.

The majestic Kelpies rise high into the sky.

Keeping in touch with small communities is important.
Even if that means landing on the beach.

Fishing has always been very important in Scotland.

We love our sports. Come on Scotland!

History and loyalty are very important to the Scots.

It looks like evening is coming to Stalker castle in the Highlands.

The sun is setting over Edinburgh Castle.
That means its bed time for me. I have
really enjoyed telling you all about
Scotland. I hope to see you soon.

Night Night.

Collect them all and support your child's learning.
Why not get an eBook for their device to encourage independent learning and reading?
Check us out at ahjamieson.com